How to Make a Rope Swing
© Shawn Fisher
Trade Edition, 2014
ISBN 978-1-63092-062-3

HOW TO MAKE A ROPE SWING

A full-length play

by Shawn Fisher

As part of a two-company rolling world premiere,

HOW TO MAKE A ROPE SWING was originally produced by SALT LAKE ACTING COMPANY (Keven Myhre and Cynthia Flemming, Executive Producers) opening on February 6, 2013. It was directed by Adrianne Moore; the set design was by Keven Myhre; the costume design was by Kevin Alberts; the lighting design was by Jesse Portillo; the sound design was by Josh Martin. The cast was as follows:

ARTHUR "BO" WELLS...............Glenn Turner
MRS. DELORES WRIGHT............Jayne Luke
"MICK" McCAFFREY.................Lucas Bybee

and

HOW TO MAKE A ROPE SWING was originally produced by CAPE MAY STAGE (Roy Steinberg, Producing Artistic Director) opening on May 17, 2013 after an initial staged reading on October 17, 2011. The production was directed by Roy Steinberg; the set design was by Spencer Potter; the costume design was by Michele Sinacore; the lighting design was by Cyrus Newitt. The cast was as follows:

MRS. DELORES WRIGHT...........Lynn Cohen
ARTHUR "BO" WELLS...............Barry Phillips
"MICK" McCAFFREY.................Ben Rosenblatt

CHARACTERS:

ARTHUR "BO" WELLS, a black custodian in his seventies.

"MICK" McCAFFREY, a white custodian in his twenties.

MRS. DELORES WRIGHT, a white town matriarch in her eighties.

TIME:

Mid Fall, 2002.

PLACE:

An old elementary schoolhouse in a rural New Jersey town near the Delaware Bay.

How to Make a Rope Swing

ACT 1, SCENE 1

(An old elementary school classroom in a small town in South Jersey. It is snowing. The room is being prepared for demolition. Old desks, boxes, a teacher's desk, a record player and miscellaneous supplies are throughout the room. Decades of class photos, some black and white and others in color, line the walls and fill boxes. A door with a frosted window reads "Grade 5" in reverse. A second door leads to the kitchen, basement and a fire exit. ARTHUR is neatly dressed in custodial attire and wears a bowtie. MICK is in similar clothes, except the bowtie, although sloppy and youthful. An unlit cigarette dangles from his lips or is tucked behind his ear most of the time. MICK has some food and drink and occasionally snacks. ARTHUR has a thermos and cup of coffee. He occasionally refers to a clipboard, inventorying the room. ARTHUR and MICK are packing up.)

MICK: So you're trying to tell me that you are basically, you are like the Jackie Robinson of the Oakbranch Public School System.

ARTHUR: Jackie Robinson?

MICK: Yeah.

ARTHUR: I said I was ONE of the first. Started here in '52. But they said because I been here longer than anybody, *I* get to choose the name.

MICK: *You* get to name the new school?

ARTHUR: Yup.

MICK: Anything you want?

ARTHUR: Yup.

MICK: So you could name it after yourself?

ARTHUR: *(pause)* Yes I could.

MICK: Bo Wells Elementary?

ARTHUR: Yes I could! Probably will. But I'll use my proper name. Arthur Wells Elementary. More dignified. With a statue out front. *(poses as if sweeping a floor)* Me sweepin' like this. *(laughs)*

MICK: Won't the old lady have something to say about it?

ARTHUR: Prob'ly. She's paying for it. But I'm still pickin' the name.

MICK: You mean you're gonna *suggest* the name!

ARTHUR: Fine, but suggesting is practically picking and still that's something. That is something isn't it?

MICK: It's something. *(pause)* So if you weren't the first then why are they letting you do it?

ARTHUR: The first person ain't here to pick the name-

MICK: Suggest

ARTHUR: The first person ain't here to *suggest* the name, right? So I was second, by three days, but they gave me points for not dying! *(beat)* If I said I was the

first then your Jackie Robinson question would not sound so ignorant. But as I am the second... you sound ignorant.

MICK: Shoot, I ain't ignorant.

ARTHUR: Now, if you'd stop distracting me and what-not, maybe we can get all this packed up before the snow gets too bad. *(looking out a window)* You believe this? They said it was gonna be nothin' but rain.

MICK: I don't know Bo... I might have to take you off my list of role models, now that I know you're not like Jackie Robinson.

ARTHUR: You still on that? You even know who that was?

MICK: Of course I know-

ARTHUR: *Who* he then?

MICK: He's-

ARTHUR: *Who* he then?! *(beat)* See you don't know.

MICK: I know. Everybody knows who Jackie Robinson was.

ARTHUR: If you know, then say something that isn't dumb. Go'head.

(MICK writes "Jackie Robinson" on the chalkboard.)

MICK: My report is on Jackie Robinson, one of the greatest men in American history-

ARTHUR: Just flappin' your gums. Trying to look smart. *(laughs)*

MICK: *(still reciting)* Jackie Robinson broke the color barrier in Major League Baseball. While all other African-American ball players were relegated to the so-called Negro Leagues-

ARTHUR: Oh "relegated"? You learn that in them classes of yours? Just 'cause you took two years of college-

MICK: While all other African-American ball players were re-le-gat-ed... You can look that up old man-

ARTHUR: Oh I know what it means.

MICK: ...to the Negro Leagues, Jackie was able to smash down the walls that separated men by color-

ARTHUR: Oh you on a first name basis even, callin' him Jackie. I see. "Smash down the walls?" Please. He didn't smash nothin'. Just 'cause he was the first, don't mean he *broke* the color barrier. He did no breakin'. Now Larry Doby... He did some breaking. *(pause, no response)* You don't know who Larry Doby is? *(He changes the writing to "Larry Doby")* Now start talking. *(laughs)*

MICK: *(pause)* So what! I don't know who Larry Doby was.

ARTHUR: *Is...* You don't know who he *is*. He ain't dead yet. Don't go killing him off before his time. Now who he is, is the second one to play in the Major Leagues. But he was the first one to break, or should I say, smash the color barrier.

9

MICK: Not Robinson?

ARTHUR: Nope.

MICK: Wasn't he first?

ARTHUR: Yup.

MICK: Wasn't he black?

ARTHUR: Come on now!

MICK: Huh. He did play baseball, right?

ARTHUR: Awww, you are getting dumber with every word you say. It's like with each syllable that you breathe out, you leak a couple IQ points. *(beat)* Yeah, he played ball, and he was first, and he was black. *(pause)* He was the "right kind" of black. The "right kind of negro" they said. See, he been to college. And he talked... he talked like your folk.

MICK: My folk? Shoot. My folk farmed oysters down on the bay. They didn't sound like they been to college. They sound like they got socked in the mouth and came up missing a few teeth. Like my Aunt Margie... She looked just like a fat sweaty little sunburned jack-o-lantern. *(pause)* So you're saying he wasn't "black" black.

ARTHUR: Oh don't go black-blacking on me! You don't know a damn thing about black-black. Let me tell you something. Everybody knows that the greatest ball club of all time was the 1935 Pittsburgh Crawfords of the Negro Leagues. Right? Everybody with half a brain knows that.

MICK: I didn't know that.

ARTHUR: My point exactly. They were called the "Yankees of Black Baseball" which was a generous compliment to the Yankees of white baseball. Oscar Charleston, Cool Papa Bell, Ted "Double Duty" Radcliffe... I's just five years old but I knew every one of 'em. But see, that didn't matter, because they weren't allowed to play the white Yankees. They didn't get to play in the real World Series. *(pause)* That's where the other brother comes in, round 'bout *(beat)* thirteen years later.

MICK: Larry Doby.

ARTHUR: La-rry Do-by! That's right! He did the breakin'. Weren't no question when he did it neither. Fourth game of the '48 series. That's the World Series. The *white* one. Indians-Braves. Doby step up, people calling him coon, jackamammy and few names I won't repeat. They scared of the *black boogie-man*, see. Every time he step up half the place'd boo and hiss and the rest'd go out for a hotdog. I'll tell you what, he made them hotdog vendors rich just by stepping up to the plate! *(laughs)* But then... *(takes an old spanking paddle out of a box and mimes a batter)*...with one swing, one mighty swing, they's choking on them dogs. CRACK! *(swings, whistles and gestures the path of a baseball)* Four hundred, four fifty, maybe even five hundred feet of screaming baseball later and he changes some minds! From then on, people were still scared of him. But it wasn't the black boogieman no more. Nah. Now they were scared of that mighty *mighty* swing!

MICK: *(pause)* So then you're the Larry Doby of the Oakbranch Public School System.

11

ARTHUR: Yeah that's right! I'm Larry Doby! And I'm entering the Haaaall of Fame. Me naming the school, this is my... what do they call it? My "induction" into the Hall. *(pause)* They givin' me a plaque too.

MICK: No shit, a plaque? Aw man, they ain't givin' you a plaque.

ARTHUR: Probably they will. With my name on it, you know? *(He mimes a plaque with his hands.)* "Arthur Wells welcomes you to Arthur Wells Elementary School."

MICK: You really gonna name it that? You should, see if she goes for it. Then you can name something after me. Like the lunch room.

ARTHUR: You want me to name the lunch room "McCaffrey"?

MICK: Yeah. Lunch was my favorite class. "The McCaffrey Lunch Room".

ARTHUR: That's stupid. Nobody names a lunch room.

MICK: No wait... I got it. *(pause)* "The McCaffreteria!" *(laughs)* Huh? That sounds good! You should do that, if the old lady lets you.

ARTHUR: Let's me? Look... This here school is my house now. She ain't principal here no more. She been gone for ten years. So she ain't in charge.

MICK: Yeah well she's paying for the new school, so I think that makes her in charge.

ARTHUR: They said *I'm* the one pickin' the name and *I'm* the one gonna be guest of honor at the ground breaking ceremony, so that means *I'm* in charge.

MICK: You're gonna be the guest of honor?

ARTHUR: That's right.

MICK: No shit. You scared?

ARTHUR: Scared of what?

MICK: Scared of the fact that you gotta make a speech.

ARTHUR: I don't gotta make a speech.

MICK: Yeah you do. You gotta wear a suit and you gotta make a speech.

ARTHUR: Well I ain't making a speech.

MICK: You got a suit?

ARTHUR: 'Course I got a suit.

MICK: Because you gotta look good. At a ground breaking ceremony even the shovels look good. They make 'em out of silver or gold or something. So you gotta have a suit or else the shovels will look better than you.

ARTHUR: I said I got a suit! I got two of 'em. I got a brown one for church and I got a black one for funerals.

MICK: *(pause)* Black looks better when you make a speech. *(beat)* Can I borrow the other one? The brown one? I don't have a suit.

ARTHUR: What you need a suit for?

MICK: 'Cause I wanna come see you make a speech. Can I borrow it?

ARTHUR: Boy, I don't want you stinkin' up my church clothes! And I ain't making a speech. I'll let the old lady do it.

MICK: That's a good idea. She was the old mayor's wife for all those years and she's been giving away all his money, so she's probably been to ground-breaking ceremonies before. Half the town's named after her. Wright Park. Wright Boulevard.

ARTHUR: Yeah well if she wants to give away any more money, I got a suggestion… How about the "Bo Wells Foundation for the Advancement of a new Fishin' Boat!" *(laughs)*

(MRS. WRIGHT enters, unseen. She has white hair and is confident but frail. She carries a cane but rarely uses it to walk. Her clothes are neat and practical including snow boots. She watches the two men.)

MICK: *(laughs)* I guess she never had any kids to give her money to. Probably was all dried up. Full of dust. Full of *cobwebs*, if you know what I mean. *(beat)* She was a mean old shit too. One time she made me scrape all the gum from under the desks and turn it into a sculpture of the Washington Monument, just 'cause she caught me with a wad of Hubba Bubba in my mouth. You remember Hubba Bubba? That stuff was good. Then she put it in the trophy case with my name on it for everybody to see.

(ARTHUR turns and sees MRS. WRIGHT. MICK is unaware.)

MICK: And she had this voice... like a nasty old black crow. She said to me one time, "If you insist on this oral fixation regarding the constant chewing of bubble gum, then soon it will be cigarettes, then prison then death." She didn't know what she was talking about. *(tries to light a cigarette)* Something like that can make an impression. She'd let out a screech. She'd yell-

MRS. WRIGHT: *(loudly, with intent to startle)* Mr. McCaffrey!

MICK: Shit!... *(drops his cigarette)* Hello... I mean, Good Morning... Good Morning Mrs., Principal Wright.

MRS. WRIGHT: It's afternoon Mr. McCaffrey. I see your powers of observation have not improved. I also see you have been promoted from gum chewer to cigarette smoker. You are well on your way.

MICK: Yes ma'am. *(pause)* Shit, shoot! No ma'am. I haven't been arrested yet. I'm in college now.

MRS. WRIGHT: Well, the community college is just three blocks from the county jail so the transition should be a quick one. *(beat)* So what arc you doing here? Cleaning the *cobwebs* from my school?

MICK: Well yeah we... Cobwebs?

MRS. WRIGHT: Yes. Didn't I hear you say something about cobwebs? *(long pause)* Mr. Wells, I was pleased to learn you are still working here.

ARTHUR: Pleased? For real?

MRS. WRIGHT: Of course. I wouldn't say it if it weren't true.

ARTHUR: It's just a surprise to me, that's all. In all those years you barely said nothin' to me.

MRS. WRIGHT: Why would I have done that? My job was rescuing the minds of young people and yours was making sure the toilets flushed. Your work was of no concern to me. And as you kept the toilets in generally good working order, I saw little need.

ARTHUR: Was there a compliment mixed in there, ma'am?

MRS. WRIGHT: If you insist.

MICK: Bo, I don't think that was a comp-

MRS. WRIGHT: Mr. McCaffrey! I do not believe you were being addressed.

MICK: Uhhh, I'm... gonna go... check the truck... *(pause, exits)*

MRS. WRIGHT: For someone who spent so much time trying to avoid doing his school work, I am surprised to see Mr. McCaffrey employed.

ARTHUR: He's alright. Slow as molasses, but alright.

MRS. WRIGHT: If you say so. *(Long pause. She examines the room.)* This place has certainly fallen from its former glory... since I left.

(She needs to rest her legs and finds a place to sit. ARTHUR attempts to assist her. She resists.)

ARTHUR: Well ma'am, old age will do that.

MRS. WRIGHT: Will it? *(pause)* So Mr. Wells, it seems you are to assist me in the naming of the new building. You know, I selected you personally. Did they tell you that?

ARTHUR: Well, actually no they-

MRS. WRIGHT: They asked me to do it, and I insisted that you be part of the discussion.

ARTHUR: They asked you? By yourself?!

MRS. WRIGHT: Of course. I'm paying for it. Who else are they going to ask?

ARTHUR: Well, I don't know what to say.

MRS. WRIGHT: Good, because I'm not interested in your gratitude. I selected you because you were the right person for the task.

ARTHUR: Well I been here a long time... and I know the ins and the outs of this here school. Came in 1952. I was just a handyman back then-

MRS. WRIGHT: Save it Mr. Wells. I do not need to hear your curriculum vitae.

ARTHUR: Seven am until four pm with an hour lunch break. That's eight hours of work. A full day.

MRS. WRIGHT: If you say so. When I worked here I arrived at seven am to unlock the doors and departed at seven pm every day.

ARTHUR: Well then it seems that rescuing the minds of young people is more time consuming than making sure the toilets flush.

MRS. WRIGHT: It does seem so doesn't it?

(MICK enters covered in snow. He raises his hand.)

ARTHUR: What are you doing?

MICK: One, I wanted to tell you the truck is full and the roads are getting real bad, and second, I want to apologize in advance to Mrs. Wright for the next thing that I do or say that is either stupid, rude or generally offensive to your opinion of me.

MRS. WRIGHT: *(sighs)* Well Mr. McCaffrey, I think that statement was it.

MICK: Good! "A good plan makes a good man!" It's what you always said Principal Wright. Is it not? I was just planning ahead! *(exits)*

(ARTHUR grabs one last box and starts to exit. MRS. WRIGHT sits. She looks in a drawer and reminisces.)

ARTHUR: Well, Mrs. Wright, I guess I need to get on out of here and over to the warehouse. *(long pause. MRS. WRIGHT ignores him.)* I gotta lock up the building. *(long pause)* Can I walk you out?

MRS. WRIGHT: Mr. Wells, for decades I was the last person to leave this building. I know, when locking the front door, the key must be pulled upwards and slightly to the right to allow it to turn. The lock on the back fire exit can only be engaged if the handle is slightly compressed and the third window in the second grade classroom cannot be adequately secured unless a board, two feet three inches long is placed in the window track. During all my years there was not a single crime recorded on these grounds. You may go on your way and I will be sure to secure the building, as I have always done.

ARTHUR: But-

MRS. WRIGHT: As I have always done!

ARTHUR: *(pause)* Alright ma'am. You're right. This here is your house. I's just the help! *(pause)* I'll see you at four o'clock then. Don't be too long in here. OK?

MRS. WRIGHT: I will leave when I am ready!

ARTHUR: I meant on account of the snow.

MRS. WRIGHT: I have my snow boots on Mr. Wells!

ARTHUR: Well... what do you know? I see that now. I'm sorry I hadn't noticed that. Those are some fine boots. I should have noticed them boots.

(ARTHUR begins to leave then stops.)

ARTHUR: By the way, there's a snow shovel around back, in the shed. You wait much longer, you gonna need it.

21

(ARTHUR exits. MRS. WRIGHT examines the room. She erases the board. She crosses to an old record player and plays a record of children's music, perhaps "Ten Little Indians". She sits at the desk, lays her head down and closes her eyes as memories fill her. Pause. The lights begin to flicker. Power outage. The record player slows to a stop. Blackout.)

ACT 1, SCENE 2

(Later that evening. It is dark outside and the lights are still out. MRS. WRIGHT still sits with her head down, asleep. The sound of a door offstage. ARTHUR enters. He is cold. He sees MRS. WRIGHT and freezes.)

ARTHUR: Mrs. Wright? *(no response)* Mrs. Wright? *(no response)* Delores!

(MRS. WRIGHT awakens abruptly. She is confused.)

MRS. WRIGHT: What?! What do you want? *(calling to her late husband)* Edward? *(pause)* Why did you turn out the lights?

ARTHUR: Delores? You alright?

MRS. WRIGHT: You startled me, Edward.

ARTHUR: It's me, Arthur. Arthur Wells. But don't worry about it.

MRS. WRIGHT: Arthur?

ARTHUR: That's right. My name is Arthur. But it's alright, we all forget sometimes. Nothing wrong with forgetting.

MRS. WRIGHT: Mr...

ARTHUR: It's alright Delores.

MRS. WRIGHT: *(pause, realizing)* What makes you think that we are on a first name basis Mr. Wells?

ARTHUR: I'm sorry... I heard you-

MRS. WRIGHT: You heard me what?

ARTHUR: Well ma'am, you were calling me Edward.

MRS. WRIGHT: I most certainly was not!

ARTHUR: Yes ma'am you were. I heard you clear as day, even with my ears froze off like this. I could still hear you clear as day.

MRS. WRIGHT: I know who you are perfectly, Mr. Wells. I certainly would not call you by your first name let alone by the wrong first name.

ARTHUR: Well then you must have been calling somebody else. Somebody named Edward.

MRS. WRIGHT: What is it you want? I thought you left.

ARTHUR: Yes I did.

MRS. WRIGHT: Then what, may I ask, are you doing here? We were to reconvene at the Oakbranch Public School warehouse. Were we not?

ARTHUR: Yes ma'am we were. Four o'clock.

MRS. WRIGHT: Well then, Perhaps you didn't trust that I could secure the building as we discussed.

ARTHUR: Well Mrs. Wright-

MRS. WRIGHT: Because I assure you, I can do so with my eyes closed. Why is it so dark in here?

ARTHUR: Mrs. Wright-

MRS. WRIGHT: I was just about to leave, after first making final rounds through the building-

ARTHUR: Ma'am-

MRS. WRIGHT: ...to make sure that all is secure and safe. Fire extinguishers, exit signs, kitchen stove and so forth-

ARTHUR: Delores!

MRS. WRIGHT: *(pause)* Why did you call me Delores again Mr. Wells? I thought I had been abundantly clear about such informality.

ARTHUR: It's nighttime. You been here for hours.

MRS. WRIGHT: I most certainly have not! I just sat down here a moment ago. It is no later than two thirty. It says so right there on the clock. I assume that even custodians know how to tell time.

ARTHUR: Yup. We also know... and I'll go real slow here, so you can stick with me... that if the electricity goes out, electrical things, including clocks, generally speaking, stop workin'.

MRS. WRIGHT: Why are you talking to me like that?

ARTHUR: But that's something that only many years of custodial training and experience can prepare you to know. Don't feel bad. It's complicated. My expertise tells me that the power went out 'round about *(looks at clock)* two twenty-seven.

MRS. WRIGHT: Mr. Wells, I don't like your tone.

(MRS. WRIGHT attempts to stand but becomes light-headed and must sit again. ARTHUR attempts to help.)

MRS. WRIGHT: I can handle myself!

ARTHUR: *(pause)* I know you can. I was just worried... And then you were just sitting there. *(pause)* I was afraid you were...

MRS. WRIGHT: *(pause)* What? You were afraid I was what? *(beat)* Because I am most certainly not dead yet.

ARTHUR: That's not what I was-

MRS. WELLS: Yes it was. And I am not... quite. People have been showing up at my house for months checking to see if I am dead yet, so I know what it looks like. I told all of them that they aren't in my will, but they keep coming anyway. They just smile and pretend like they didn't hear me. Bringing me casseroles, cookies. That won't keep me alive. It will just make me look fat when I am lying in my casket. So I send them away with their junk food and I continue to take care of myself, as I have always done.

ARTHUR: That's good to hear. *(pause)* I waited for you at the warehouse but you never showed. I couldn't call, so I come here to check.

MRS. WRIGHT: Well you wasted your time. So I dozed off for a few hours. I was tired. Everybody dozes off once in a while when they get tired. You doze off once in a while. I bet you have a little cot hidden away in a store room somewhere so you can take a nap in the middle of the work day. Your kind have a propensity to do that.

ARTHUR: My kind?

MRS. WRIGHT: Yes, custodians.

ARTHUR: *(pause)* You a firecracker, lady. You always were. And now I'm gonna get in trouble, comin' here 'cause of you. Me and Mick borrowed the truck to see if you were stuck on the side of the road somewhere in the snow.

MRS. WRIGHT: So where is Mr. McCaffrey then?

ARTHUR: That's the problem. He's with the truck, stuck on the side of the road in the snow. *(pause)* He's diggin' it out and he'll come pick us up when he does. We slid off the road on Butler Avenue. I told you that truck is no good in the snow. If you had just did what I told you-

MRS. WRIGHT: How did you get here?

ARTHUR: I walked.

MRS. WRIGHT: You did not. Butler Avenue must be miles from here.

ARTHUR: Yes it is.*(pause)* But I'll survive. It's not that far.

MRS. WRIGHT: No, of course it isn't. Well... Then I guess... I still have my car.

ARTHUR: Your car ain't goin' nowhere 'til the plow truck come around. Can't even make it out the driveway.

MRS. WRIGHT: Well then you are going to have to push. *(exits abruptly)*

ARTHUR: I'm gonna have to push? I ain't gonna push! Who you think you are lady? Telling me I gotta push. I don't even know if I got any toes left. Can't feel a damn thing down there. I ain't pushing nothin' 'til I figure out if my toes been froze off.

(MRS. WRIGHT re-enters)

MRS. WRIGHT: Where's my car?

ARTHUR: Did you see two piles of snow out there?

MRS. WRIGHT: Yes.

ARTHUR: One of em's your car. The other one is a pile of garbage and I ain't fixin' to dig out either one of 'em right now.

MRS. WRIGHT: I am not going to sit here-

ARTHUR: Yeah well stand if you want. But I am sitting right here until my toes come back to life and Mick shows up.

MRS. WRIGHT: And it's cold in here.

ARTHUR: There ain't no heat.

MRS. WRIGHT: Thank you for elaborating.

ARTHUR: That's on account of the electricity going out. See, the pump on the furnace… The heat just don't work without electricity.

MRS. WRIGHT: This is a fine situation.

ARTHUR: Well I ain't too happy about it myself.

(They sit. MRS. WRIGHT breathes heavily. A long uncomfortable silence follows.)

ARTHUR: Well then let's go.

MRS. WRIGHT: Go where?

ARTHUR: Let's do this.

MRS. WRIGHT: What are you talking about?

ARTHUR: We got something to do. Let's do it.

MRS. WRIGHT: I don't think-

ARTHUR: I pick Larry Doby.

MRS. WRIGHT: Larry-

ARTHUR: Yeah, Doby.

MRS. WRIGHT: What about him?

ARTHUR: That's who we should name the school after.

MRS. WRIGHT: I am not in the mood to discuss-

ARTHUR: We are stuck here for a while and I am not
    about to sit here listening to you sigh and huff and puff
    about our situation. I pick Larry Doby.

MRS. WRIGHT: You PICK? You don't get to pick anybody. You are here to discuss, suggest, confer or advise, but not to pick.

ARTHUR: Lady, what are you a human dictionary?

MRS. WRIGHT: Pardon me?

ARTHUR: You are like a walking dictionary, full of words. You just said four words that mean the same thing.

MRS. WRIGHT: Then you mean thesaurus. I am a walking thesaurus. If you are going to be offensive, at least use the right word.

ARTHUR: What's wrong with my word?

MRS. WRIGHT: There's nothing worse than somebody using lazy language.

ARTHUR: Lazy?... It's just as much work for me to talk as it is for you to talk. My word's just as good as yours.

MRS. WRIGHT: You used the wrong one. Thesaurus would have been better.

ARTHUR: Thesaurus ain't better. That's a terrible word. It's hard to say. Too many thhh's and s-s-s-ses.

MRS. WRIGHT: You should speak correctly.

ARTHUR: And it sounds like a dinosaur.

MRS. WRIGHT: A dinosaur?

ARTHUR: Yeah. You know... like a dinosaur with a large vocabulary.

MRS. WRIGHT: Are you trying to make a joke?

ARTHUR: A Tyranno-thesaurus Rex.

(MRS. WRIGHT chuckles then stops herself.)

ARTHUR: I saw that! That's what you are, a dinosaur with a large vocabulary! Ha!

MRS. WRIGHT: You're calling me a dinosaur?

ARTHUR: I was making a joke.

MRS. WRIGHT: You are being insulting.

ARTHUR: I am?

MRS. WRIGHT: Yes. Calling me a dinosaur.

ARTHUR: But I said with a large vocabulary.

MRS. WRIGHT: What does that have to do with it?

ARTHUR: It's a compliment.

MRS. WRIGHT: A dinosaur is an insult.

ARTHUR: Not to a dinosaur.

MRS. WRIGHT: I'm not a dinosaur.

ARTHUR: Then what are you?

MRS. WRIGHT: What does that mean?

ARTHUR: Tell me what you are and I can stop calling you a dinosaur.

MRS. WRIGHT: I am not interested in your games-

ARTHUR: We saw each other every day for most of our lives, but we are basically strangers and I don't think strangers work well together.

MRS. WRIGHT: Mr. Wells-

ARTHUR: What did you do this morning?

MRS. WRIGHT: Why is that any of your-

ARTHUR: When I got up this morning, I made a tomato and cheese omelet.

MRS. WRIGHT: I don't really care about your eating habits-

ARTHUR: I tried to make it just the same way my wife used to.

MRS. WRIGHT: *(sarcastically)* That's touching.

ARTHUR: Today is our anniversary, my wife and me. Every year on our anniversary, I try and make a tomato and cheese omelet. Just like the ones she used to make. Mmmm, she made 'em good too. They were creamy but not runny. Just a little bit of brown, but not enough to make em' taste burnt. Three eggs, sharp cheddar, a little bit of chives and one fresh tomato. I try to make it every year. But either the eggs are too dry, or the cheese isn't melted and mixed in enough. I keep a close eye on it. I check the bottom to make sure it ain't getting brown or drying out. But every time-

MRS. WRIGHT: Stop fussing with it.

ARTHUR: I'm sorry?

MRS. WRIGHT: Stop fussing with the eggs.

ARTHUR: I don't fuss.

MRS. WRIGHT: Yes you do. And use a shallow pan with a low lid. You're cooking it without a lid.

ARTHUR: No I'm not.

MRS. WRIGHT: I think you are.

ARTHUR: *(pause)* Maybe I am.

MRS. WRIGHT: Little bit of butter. Turn down the heat. Turn it way down. Pour the egg in. And leave it alone. For five minutes do not even look at it. You are messing with it too much.

ARTHUR: Is that so?

MRS. WRIGHT: Yes it is.

ARTHUR: Hmph. *(pause)* After that, I went over to the cemetery to visit my wife. I dug up her flowers. Chrysanthemums. Yellow ones. Those were her favorite. So every Spring, on her birthday, I plant 'em at the cemetery, and then on our anniversary, in the Fall, I dig 'em up. I bring them home and keep them in the window.

MRS. WRIGHT: You never remarried?

ARTHUR: No I didn't.

MRS. WRIGHT: That's too bad.

ARTHUR: Why is that bad?

MRS. WRIGHT: A man needs to be married. Or else he will get himself into trouble.

ARTHUR: I *am* married.

MRS. WRIGHT: I mean he shouldn't be alone. A man needs a wife.

ARTHUR: I can wait.

MRS. WRIGHT: *(pause)* I knew Marian.

ARTHUR: I know.

MRS. WRIGHT: I worked with her.

ARTHUR: I know.

MRS. WRIGHT: In this very room.

ARTHUR: You were still a teacher then.

MRS. WRIGHT: I was. And so was she.

ARTHUR: Naah. Not here she wasn't. They wouldn't let her. They called her a "Teacher's Helper". She didn't want to come here. But they moved her from the colored school anyway. Her and them seven children. The first seven to come over. They didn't want to come here neither. *(pause, smiles)* But I did. I always wanted to be where she was. Keep her close. I was afraid she'd come to her senses and realize she's too good for

34

me. So after she come here, after three days, they let me switch buildings. *(pause)* I don't know what she was thinking, marrying a man like me. She college educated, with a real important job and I convince her that a handyman'd make a good husband. "Who you gonna pay to fix the plumbing?", I said. "And when a doorknob come loose, who you gonna pay to fix it on a teacher's salary from over at the colored school?" Again and again she turn me down. 'Til one day she come up to me and say she got a problem. She say the light in the kitchen stop working and could I come over and fix it. So I do. It just wasn't screwed in tight enough 'sall. So I fix it for her. *(pause, smiles)* But, I make it look reeeeal hard. Get out all my tools. Lay 'em out on the table. Spend a half hour on that loose light bulb. And to thank me, she offer me some cake. Some *good* cake too. So I go into the bathroom to wash my hands, I gotta make a good impression, and clean hands is part of that. So while I'm in there, *(whispers)* I make sure she can't hear nothin', and I loosen up the drain pipe... under the sink. *(chuckles)* Yup. Just a little bit. So it drip... drip... drip. Guess what happens the next day? *(in a woman's voice)* "Bo, could you come over and fix my sink?" *(his voice)* "Sure thing Miss Marian, I think I could find some time to do that for you. So long as you got more of that fine cake." Then, you know what happen? *(feigning surprise)* The next day the hinge on the cabinet come loose! Then it's a floorboard! Then a door latch! *(woman's voice)* "Bo, I think my whole house is fallin' apart. Can you come over again?" See I was smart right? I had her right where I wanted her. She *need* me to be around. So I convince her to marry me. *(pause)* I didn't find out until our wedding night when she confess... She knew it all along. She knew it was me messing up those things. Shoot, she played me the

35

whole time. Then you know what she told me? She told me, she had went and loosened up that light bulb in the first place! *(laughs)* Believe that? That right there… That's the kind of woman you wanna marry.

MRS. WRIGHT: I suppose.

ARTHUR: It's the truth. I was never gonna pull anything over on her. I was trouble when I was a kid. In trouble with the law. Nothing big, but always something. And she knew it. I said to her, "I ain't that person no more." And she said, "part of you is." And I said, "but most of me ain't!" And she said, "I know… and that's the part of you I want." *(pause)* So she keep me straight. Just like those children… her students. But then they move her here, to the white school. Here she was just a… just a "nanny". But over at the colored school, she was a great teacher.

MRS. WRIGHT: That's why she was chosen to teach here, in this school. That's why she was first.

ARTHUR: I said they didn't let her teach. At the colored school the kids all wanted Miss Marian. That's what they called her there. But then they bring her here and change who she was. Start calling by her fancy name… Mrs. Wells. Said it was *civilized*. *(beat)* But all they let her do was walk those seven children to the bathroom. Told her to make sure they didn't pee on the floor. *(pause) Civilized. (pause)* She said some teachers, they treat her real bad too. Ordered her around… Never let her talk. She would come home with tears in her eyes.

MRS. WRIGHT: I didn't like Marian.

ARTHUR: I know.

MRS. WRIGHT: And she didn't like me much either.

ARTHUR: Much? *(pause)* You were mean.

MRS. WRIGHT: I was not. I just didn't want her here any more than she wanted to be here. She always wanted to do things her way.

ARTHUR: 'Cause her way was the better way. You know it was.

MRS. WRIGHT: It was my classroom.

ARTHUR: Says who?

MRS. WRIGHT: Said the Mayor. He made the rules, I just followed.

ARTHUR: Awww Mrs. Wright, you never just followed in your life. This here was your classroom. You made the rules. You still makin' the rules in here.

MRS. WRIGHT: There could only be one teacher.

ARTHUR: Yeah, and they pick the wrong one.

MRS. WRIGHT: What makes you so sure?

ARTHUR: 'Cause she the one who ain't here no more.

MRS. WRIGHT: *(pause)* What does that have to do with it?

ARTHUR: You tell me.

MRS. WRIGHT: I don't know anything about any of that.

ARTHUR: Yeah I know. Been hearing that for years.

MRS. WRIGHT: It was a long time ago.

ARTHUR: Long time? She died fifty years ago, but just this morning, I was having a *sweet* dream about her and me. I won't tell you the details, but I promise you it was sweet. But then I wake up, and I look for her next to me, but she ain't there. I realize it's just a dream. That happened *this morning*. And this morning weren't a long time ago at all. *(pause)* You ever have dreams about your husband? And then you wake up and realize he's gone?

MRS. WRIGHT: That's personal.

ARTHUR: Tell me about them personal dreams.

MRS. WRIGHT: You don't listen do you?

ARTHUR: Oh I hear you. Tell me about them dreams.

MRS. WRIGHT: Can we just move on to our business?

ARTHUR: *(moves close to MRS. WRIGHT.)* Depends on how good the dream is. You tell me... and I'll go sit over there and leave you alone.

MRS. WRIGHT: *(shifts uncomfortably)* You are impossible.

ARTHUR: That's what Marian used to say. *(beat, moves very close)* Go ahead. And I'll leave you be.

MRS. WRIGHT: Fine. *(dismissive)* We are sitting under a tree. Having a picnic... like we used to do. That's my dream.

ARTHUR: *(pause)* That's it? That's your dream? That dream's no good.

MRS. WRIGHT: Well there's more to it than that. But I don't feel like-

ARTHUR: Well tell it!

MRS. WRIGHT: *(pause)* We are enjoying ourselves with some sandwiches and some cake. And then it's interrupted. It turns into a nightmare after that and I'd rather not talk about that part.

ARTHUR: That's the good stuff. Come on.

MRS. WRIGHT: *(pause)* Edward and I are sitting under the tree-

ARTHUR: You say Edward? That's your husband's name?

MRS. WRIGHT: Yes. And so Edward is-

ARTHUR: See I knew you were screamin' Edward!

MRS. WRIGHT: Are you going to allow me to finish my story or aren't you?

ARTHUR: I'll be quiet.

MRS. WRIGHT: *(pause)* It's sunny and beautiful. I can hear children playing. I look up and see the tree above me is endless… branches reaching as far as the eye can see, and children are swinging from every branch. Laughing, singing. *(pause)* Then the sky starts to get cloudy. The wind begins to blow and the children clutch the ropes of their swings. They begin to cry and the wind blows them harder and faster and higher. Then one of them gets blown so hard that the knot at the top of the rope swing gets pulled loose and the swing breaks free sending the child through the sky and to the ground far below. Then a second child. And another… and another. Until, amidst the thunder and lightning, it begins to rain children. Thousands of them. Then I turn to Edward and say "Edward, do something. They are falling! Catch them!" And I see him just lying there enjoying his cake with a big smile, like nothing is happening.

ARTHUR: *(pause)* That there's a messed up dream.

MRS. WRIGHT: You told me to tell you. I didn't want to.

ARTHUR: You know what the problem is with that dream?

MRS. WRIGHT: Now you are going to critique my dream?

ARTHUR: No. I am going to fix it. See, I'm a handyman. I fix things. The problem is with them rope swings. They weren't tied right to the tree. See, I know how to make a rope swing. What that dream needs is a handy-man. So here, do this. Close your eyes.

MRS. WRIGHT: Mr. Wells-

ARTHUR: Close 'em. Just do what I'm askin'.

(MRS. WRIGHT closes her eyes reluctantly.)

ARTHUR: Picture that dream of yours. Describe it to me.

MRS. WRIGHT: *(opens her eyes)* I am not going to-

ARTHUR: I'll fix it!

MRS. WRIGHT: This is silly. *(closes her eyes)* We are sitting under the tree. Having a pic-

ARTHUR: Describe the tree, exactly how you see it.

MRS. WRIGHT: It's a large Oak tree. Ancient. And on the side of the tree is a black burned scar.

ARTHUR: A scar?

MRS. WRIGHT: It was where the farmhands would build a fire to cook meals.

ARTHUR: Farmhands, huh? What's it look like?

MRS. WRIGHT: It's an old scar. Two hundred years, maybe three. And as the trunk grew larger and thicker, it started to close over the old fire mark, making the scar deeper but harder to see.

ARTHUR: You talking about the big tree over there by the river?

MRS. WRIGHT: Yes.

ARTHUR: I know that tree. Everybody knows that tree. That's the "Slave Tree". I know that scar too. That's where the slaves cooked.

MRS. WRIGHT: Yes... That's what I said.

ARTHUR: No you didn't. *(pause)* Go 'head, finish the dream.

MRS. WRIGHT: The tree blocks the wind and the branches shade us from the sun. It is the perfect day.

ARTHUR: This is when you see the children.

MRS. WRIGHT: Yes. They are swinging, laughing.

ARTHUR: And then the sky goes dark, right?

MRS. WRIGHT: Yes. And the wind blows, and I look up to the branches-

ARTHUR: And you see all the children.

MRS. WRIGHT: Yes.

ARTHUR: And they are scared.

MRS. WRIGHT: Yes.

ARTHUR: They are being blown around.

MRS. WRIGHT: Yes.

ARTHUR: And there I am sitting on a branch.

MRS. WRIGHT: Yes... What? No!

ARTHUR: Yes I am sitting on a branch and I got wings.

MRS. WRIGHT: That isn't in the dream.

ARTHUR: Put it in. I am sitting there on a branch with wings.

MRS. WRIGHT: That's absurd.

ARTHUR: Yeah, your dream was so normal to begin with! Keep your eyes closed. So I got my wings and I fly up to one of the kids and I say "Don't worry kiddo... Bo got ya."

MRS. WRIGHT: You can't just put yourself in the middle of my dream.

ARTHUR: Close 'em. And then real fast, I fix the rope. I tie a clove hitch and then two half hitches just like them oystermen use. Then I fly to the next kid and then the next until finally just as the wind gets real bad I finish the last one. They are swinging all over the place, but they hang on tight and they don't go nowhere. Those swings hold tight. Now tell me what happens in the dream next?

MRS. WRIGHT: I don't know. The story is different now. You changed it.

ARTHUR: See? It's workin'. What happens next?

MRS. WRIGHT: They hold on?

ARTHUR: Right! And?

MRS. WRIGHT: And then the wind starts to die down.

ARTHUR: They safe now?

MRS. WRIGHT: Sure, Fine but-

ARTHUR: See Bo Wells knows how to make a rope swing. Bo Wells knows how to tie a knot.

MRS. WRIGHT: But that's not all.

ARTHUR: I took care of them kids. Next time you dream it, they safe.

MRS. WRIGHT: There's another part in the dream-

ARTHUR: But this is the new dream. This one is different.

MRS. WRIGHT: But there's another part.

ARTHUR: Them kids are safe, right?

MRS. WRIGHT: But in the old dream-

ARTHUR: But this is the new dream.

MRS. WRIGHT: There's still one left-

ARTHUR: That's the old dream.

MRS. WRIGHT: There's still one person left.

ARTHUR: But that person is OK. That person is safe now.

MRS. WRIGHT: Hanging there on that rope swing. But she's not OK. She got tangled up-

ARTHUR: It don't matter.

MRS. WRIGHT: In the rope swing. She fell off and got caught. By the leg-

ARTHUR: Mrs. Wright… it don't matter!

MRS. WRIGHT: And she-

ARTHUR: It don't matter!

MRS. WRIGHT: She died-

ARTHUR: It's just an old dream.

MRS. WRIGHT: And she is just hanging there.

ARTHUR: She ain't real and she didn't die 'cause I saved her this time.

MRS. WRIGHT: And-

ARTHUR: I saved her!

MRS. WRIGHT: *(pause)* OK.

ARTHUR: *(long pause)* Why you dream her like that?

MRS. WRIGHT: I don't know.

ARTHUR: Why you dream her up in a tree?

MRS. WRIGHT: I can't help it. It's just a dream I have.

ARTHUR: But why you have THAT dream?

MRS. WRIGHT: Why does anybody have any dream?

ARTHUR: No. Uh uh. That ain't just any dream.

MRS. WRIGHT: Of course it is.

ARTHUR: You listen to me! That ain't any dream. What you come here for?

MRS. WRIGHT: I'm sorry I told you.

ARTHUR: Whatchu come here for?! *(pause, no answer)* How did Marian die?

MRS. WRIGHT: I wasn't there.

ARTHUR: How did she die?

MRS. WRIGHT: I don't-

ARTHUR: HOW SHE DIE?!

MRS. WRIGHT: She drowned.

ARTHUR: Right! How she drown?

MRS. WRIGHT: I don't know.

ARTHUR: Yes you do.

MRS. WRIGHT: No.

ARTHUR: It was in the paper. Front page. What it say?

MRS. WRIGHT: She drowned.

ARTHUR: HOW SHE DROWN?!

MRS. WIRGHT: I DON'T KNOW!

ARTHUR: In the river right?

MRS. WRIGHT: Yes.

ARTHUR: Middle of the night.

MRS. WRIGHT: Evidently.

ARTHUR: And she been drinking.

MRS. WRIGHT: That's what they said. That's what the paper said.

ARTHUR: And she went crazy.

MRS. WRIGHT: That's what it said.

ARTHUR: Out of control. They wrote "a colored woman was stumblin' down the street like a dog with rabies."

MRS. WRIGHT: I remember the quote.

ARTHUR: Then she stumble down to the river and dive in.

MRS. WRIGHT: She was reckless.

ARTHUR: Went for a swim. Outa her mind.

MRS. WRIGHT: She should have known better.

ARTHUR: She couldn't swim.

MRS. WRIGHT: I guess that's why she drowned.

ARTHUR: No.

MRS. WRIGHT: She should have stayed out of the water.

ARTHUR: I said she couldn't swim! She was afraid of the water. She'd close her eyes goin' over a bridge, she so afraid. She never been within fifty yards of the side of that river. She didn't go for a swim! She couldn't. She wouldn't!

MRS. WRIGHT: Well then... maybe she...

ARTHUR: What?! Maybe she what?!

MRS. WRIGHT: Maybe she wanted to-

ARTHUR: She didn't want to! Don't you say that. I know her. Don't you ever say that.

MRS. WRIGHT: She was upset.

ARTHUR: Who found her?

MRS. WRIGHT: I don't know.

ARTHUR: Yes you do. Who found her?!

MRS. WRIGHT: The police I think.

ARTHUR: No, *I* found her.

MRS. WRIGHT: OK.

ARTHUR: They never wrote that in the paper.

MRS. WRIGHT: Did it matter who found her?

ARTHUR: They didn't write that I found her with her head underwater.

MRS. WRIGHT: Mr. Wells-

ARTHUR: Or that her hands and arms were stuck down in the mud up to her elbows like she was trying to push herself above the water.

MRS. WRIGHT: It was a horrible accident.

ARTHUR: Or that-

MRS. WRIGHT: Mr. Wells, don't-

ARTHUR: Or that she was-

MRS. WRIGHT: Don't do this.

ARTHUR: Her foot was wrapped up in the old rope swing. Just like in your dream. She was hanging by the ankle with her head under the water. Her hands trying to push her out, so she could breathe, but they just sank deeper in the mud. She was hanging from that old rope swing... just like in your dream.

MRS. WRIGHT: *(pause)* It was just a dream.

ARTHUR: Nah. You know something. Or you hear something. Or you see something. Fifty years ago, you know something.

MRS. WRIGHT: I don't... I can't remember anything. It was just an accident. A horrible accident.

ARTHUR: That's what they always said.

MRS. WRIGHT: She wasn't thinking. She was upset.

ARTHUR: I know she was.

MRS. WRIGHT: And she was drunk.

ARTHUR: She earned that drunk! Sometimes nothing but bein' drunk gonna make you feel better. And that night, she earned it didn't she?

MRS. WRIGHT: I suppose she did. That was the day she lost her job.

ARTHUR: She didn't lose it. They took it. She the first in her family who didn't work on the farms or the boats or in some lady's kitchen. It's all she ever wanted. And they take that from her.

MRS. WRIGHT: She broke the rules.

ARTHUR: What rules?

MRS. WRIGHT: She struck a child.

ARTHUR: If she hit a child it's because that child needed to be hit!

MRS. WRIGHT: *(pause)* Paddling wasn't allowed. Not up here in the North. Not in this state.

ARTHUR: No? *(pulls out the paddle.)* Then what's this?

MRS. WRIGHT: *(pause)* That's nothing. It hung on the wall. A piece of history.

ARTHUR: But this was it, wasn't it? This is the one she woulda used.

MRS. WRIGHT: Might have been. Maybe it was.

ARTHUR: So why they do it Mrs. Wright? Why they fire her? Why they take everything that mattered from her?

MRS. WRIGHT: They were protecting the children.

ARTHUR: Protecting? From what?

MRS. WRIGHT: Pain.

ARTHUR: That's a lie.

MRS. WRIGHT: Corporal punishment wasn't allowed in schools. It was illegal.

ARTHUR: Then what about this? *(holds up the paddle)*

MRS. WRIGHT: It's just a token. It wasn't real!

ARTHUR: Look at the handle.

MRS. WRIGHT: Mr. Wells-

ARTHUR: The varnish. See it? It's all worn off. From hands. From being swung... hard, like a bat. Like an old worn out baseball bat.

MRS. WRIGHT: It was just a reminder! A little fear never hurt them.

ARTHUR: A baseball bat ain't scary just hanging on a wall. It ain't scary until there's a mighty swing behind it.

MRS. WRIGHT: Mr. Wells-

ARTHUR: Did you ever swing it, Delores?

MRS. WRIGHT: Mrs. Wright.

ARTHUR: Did you ever swing it, Mrs. Wright? You a small lady, but you got fire. I bet you had a mighty swing!

MRS. WRIGHT: Paddling has been illegal here for a hundred years Mr. Wells.

ARTHUR: Did you ever give a beatin' to a child in this school?

MRS. WRIGHT: A beating?!

ARTHUR: Did you ever pick up this here paddle and beat on a student like Marian did? I bet they was afraid of that mighty swing of yours.

MRS. WRIGHT: I never *beat* a child!

ARTHUR: Did you ever paddle one, like that scary Mrs. Wells did?

MRS. WRIGHT: Don't be re-

ARTHUR: Did you ever-

MRS. WRIGHT: Mr. Wells!

ARTHUR: DID YOU EVER?!

MRS. WRIGHT: *(long pause, deliberately)* Yes. Yes we did. Sometimes. We all did.

(ARTHUR begins to leave.)

MRS. WRIGHT: But only in severe circumstances! I will not apologize for that. Those were the times!

ARTHUR: *(returning)* You said it was against the rules.

MRS. WRIGHT: We lived in South Jersey Mr. Wells. Not Philadelphia. A small town. Practical people. Farmers. Oystermen. Men of tools, not men of words! Words took too long for them. *(holds up paddle)* This, is a tool. Nothing more. And it was either this, by my skinny arm, or it was the strap when they got home, by the arm of their big strong farmer daddy. This left no scars. It was what the people knew... what they expected. It was what the *children* expected!

ARTHUR: Well they didn't expect it this time did they? Not from her.

MRS. WRIGHT: No. Not from her.

ARTHUR: *(pause)* I'm leaving. You can fend for yourself. Wait here for Mick. He'll be back soon. But then maybe he won't. But I ain't heartless. I'll tell somebody you're here, eventually, after I walk on out of here. But I don't have them good boots like you got. I just got these old shoes. Can't promise nothin' without a good pair of boots.

MRS. WRIGHT: Mr. Wells-

ARTHUR: There's some snacks in the kitchen. I found a few little packages of cookies in the pantry. Probably a couple years old. I was gonna throw 'em out, but those things never seem to go bad. Probably can still eat 'em. Enjoy 'em while you wait.

MRS. WRIGHT: Mr. Wells.

ARTHUR: Somebody'll be by soon I'm sure. Oakbranch only got one plow truck, but it'll get around to this part of town by Sunday... Monday at the latest. I'll check on you then.

MRS. WRIGHT: You'll what? You'll check... Monday? That's three days. You can't just... You must-

ARTHUR: I don't work for you no more! I don't "must" nothin'.

MRS. WRIGHT: But I... Mr. Wells... I-

ARTHUR: I'll tell somebody. I ain't heartless. I'll tell some-

MRS. WRIGHT: Arthur?

ARTHUR: *(pause, surprised)* Arthur? You call me Arthur now? No more Mr. Wells? Nobody call me Arthur. My friends call me Bo. They call me that on account of my ties. Did you know that? I always wear a bow tie, see. A regular tie is too long. It gets in the way when I'm workin'. So I wear this bowtie. It's dignified. So they call me Bo. That's something my friends know. People who aren't my friends, they call me Mr. Wells.

MRS. WRIGHT: Please don't leave Bo.

ARTHUR: We friends now?

MRS. WRIGHT: Yes.

ARTHUR: You think so?

MRS. WRIGHT: Yes. Please don't leave.

ARTHUR: You think so?

MRS. WRIGHT: I hope so.

ARTHUR: You *need* me?

MRS. WRIGHT: Yes. Please don't leave me here.

ARTHUR: *(pause)* Alright then... If you *need* me, I'll stay.

MRS. WRIGHT: I do.

ARTHUR: *(long pause)* Well then, I'ma go down the basement. There's an old generator down there. See if I can get it running, get some heat up in here. It's gonna be a cold night.

MRS. WRIGHT: Thank you.

ARTHUR: How 'bout you go find us those cookies. I missed dinner. I guess we both did. Some cookies would be real good right now... Delores.

(ARTHUR exits. MRS. WRIGHT slumps down into a chair. She weeps. Blackout.)

(END OF ACT I.)

ACT 2, SCENE 1

MRS. WRIGHT: *(in darkness)* Class, please name our first president. *(pause)* Correct. Your best penmanship please. G-E-O-R-G-E (beat) W-A-S-H-I-N-G-T-O-N.

(Lights up, tight on MRS. WRIGHT. She faces the audience directly. The rest of the stage is dark.)

Please name our sixteenth president. *(pause)* Correct. A-B-R-A... *H...A-M (beat)* L-I-N-C-O... *L...* N. Benjamin! *(pause)* Benjamin Parker! Pay attention! And keep your lips sealed. Understood? You may have been allowed such behavior at the colored school, but here at Oakbranch we are civilized! Do you understand? Say "yes ma'am"! *(pause)* Benjamin, please name our current president. *(pause)* I said current! Truman is no longer in office. Who is our new president? *(pause)* Class, our new student does not know the answer. As a result, he shall sit at the desk next to mine, hands folded until the school bell rings. *(scolding)* Mrs. Wells! Leave the boy alone! A few tears will not excuse him *or you* from the expectations of my class. In case you hadn't noticed you are not a teacher at the colored school anymore and Benjamin is no longer *your* student! He belongs to me now. Times have changed and I expect you will change with them. It's called "progress". Class... Write that down. Thanks to Mrs. Wells, it shall be our new word for the day. *(pause)* Let me tell you a story about progress. You all know the large oak tree over by the river, just beyond the school yard. Did you know it is over three hundred years old? It's the very tree from which Oakbranch took its name. My great great great grandfather would sell meat from that tree. He would walk his livestock from the farm to the tree at which time he would kill it and hang it from the strongest branch. In those days before refrigeration, meat would rot, so people would spend good money on meat that was so fresh it was still twitching... Within a few years, he built a general store, a blacksmith shop and a small inn in the shadow of that tree... and soon an entire village sprouted up. From then on, if you needed something, anything, you traveled to the "Oak Branch". From rotting meat, grew an entire community, see. That... is progress. And that... is a good thing. So Mrs. Wells, in the name of progress... remember your place! *(pause)* What is it Benjamin?! *(pause, genuinely impressed)* You remembered! Eisenhower. That is correct! You have earned one gold star for perseverance. You may return to your seat. Class, henceforth, Benjamin shall be our class scholar of the day. Now listen closely. Dwight D. Eisenhower. Your best penmanship please. D-W-I-G-H--

MICK: *(From the darkness)* Mrs. Wright?

(Lights up on the classroom. The power is still out. MRS. WRIGHT is yanked from her memories. She holds an old class photo. A man's old painting shirt hangs on her chair. MICK sits at a pupil's desk. He is wrapped in a large map of the Civil War. The occasional sound of AR-THUR banging the generator in the basement is heard.)

MICK: *(raises his hand)* Mrs. Wright?

MRS. WRIGHT: What is it Mr. McCaffrey?

MICK: What are you doing?

MRS. WRIGHT: I'm just... looking at old class photos.

MICK: Oh. Where's Bo?

MRS. WRIGHT: In the basement.

MICK: Oh. *(raises his hand again, no response)* Mrs. Wright?

MRS. WRIGHT: Yes?

MICK: Why's he in the basement?

MRS. WRIGHT: For the heat.

(MICK raises his hand again.)

MRS. WRIGHT: Yes?

MICK: Is it warmer in the basement?

MRS. WRIGHT: *(returning to her photos)* No. There's an old generator down there. He's trying to fix it. So we can have some heat.

(MICK raises his hand again.)

MRS. WRIGHT: Mr. McCaffrey, you do not need to raise your hand!

MICK: *(lowers his hand)* Um-

MRS. WRIGHT: WHAT?!

(MRS. WRIGHT feels cold and puts on the old painting shirt.)

MICK: I have a question.

MRS. WRIGHT: You don't need permission. You are not a child. You may speak freely.

MICK: OK. *(beat)* Are you mad at me?

MRS. WRIGHT: For what?

MICK: And is Bo mad at me?

MRS. WRIGHT: For what?

MICK: For getting the truck stuck?

MRS. WRIGHT: No.

MICK: And for not being able to get it out? I think I broke it. Are you mad?

MRS. WRIGHT: No.

MICK: And Bo? He seemed mad before.

MRS. WRIGHT: That's between you and him. None of my concern.

MICK: Where'd you get that shirt?

MRS. WRIGHT: From the arts and crafts box.

MICK: Is it warm?

MRS. WRIGHT: No.

MICK: Are there any more?

MRS. WRIGHT: No.

MICK: This map isn't warm at all.

MRS. WRIGHT: It's just paper.

MICK: I know. That's what I mean. What's it a map of?

MRS. WRIGHT: *(looks)* The United States during the Civil War. *(back to photos)*

MICK: How can you tell?

MRS. WRIGHT: I know what the United States looked like during the Civil War.

MICK: Really? How old were you?

(MRS. WRIGHT glares at MICK.)

MICK: *(pause then realizing)* Did you say the Civil War? Pfft. I thought you said World War wwwwwwwwww... *(pause)* Two?

MRS. WRIGHT: The map is the Civil War.

MICK: How can you tell?

MRS. WRIGHT: It has the Mason-Dixon line.

MICK: Oh. *(pause)* Which class is that one?

MRS. WRIGHT: 1953.

MICK: Is one of those my class?

MRS. WRIGHT: Most likely.

MICK: Can I look?

MRS. WRIGHT: I don't care! Do what you want.

(MICK grabs a stack of photos.)

MICK: Hey this one's from the Seventies. Look at those pants. That kid was just askin' to get beat up. "Mrs. Wright's fifth Grade Class, 1974." Hey look, that's you.

MRS. WRIGHT: Did you figure that out all by yourself?

MICK: No. It says it right here. "Mrs. Wright's fifth Grade Class, 1974."

MRS. WRIGHT: Yes, I know.

MICK: You were a teacher?

MRS. WRIGHT: Yes, a very good one.

MICK: Really? I mean... I'm sure you were. You were principal when I went here.

MRS. WRIGHT: That was after... I stopped teaching.

MICK: Oh. You didn't like it anymore?

MRS. WRIGHT: Why are you asking so many questions?!

MICK: I don't know. We don't have a T.V.

MRS. WRIGHT: Well it's irritating.

MICK: So why'd you quit?

MRS. WRIGHT: I didn't quit, I retired.

MICK: Why'd you retire then?

MRS. WRIGHT: Because they needed me to be Principal. Must you be so nosy?

MICK: I'm just wondering. A simple question.

MRS. WRIGHT: It was because they decided to come in and screw things up and try and make us teach a certain way. I didn't like it. So I retired from teaching.

MICK: You mean they fired you?

MRS. WRIGHT: No! Of course not! I was the best teacher this school ever had, bar none. I was just too old to start a whole new system. OK? Your curiosity satisfied?

MICK: Not really. But I'll shut up.

MRS. WRIGHT: Fine.

MICK: *(picks up a photo)* Hey... can I ask you something?

MRS. WRIGHT: *(sighs)* Why not?

MICK: You ever wonder about them? Ever wonder if you did good?

MRS. WRIGHT: If I did well?

MICK: Yeah. You ever wonder if all those kids ended up OK? I mean Oakbranch was a pretty screwed up place. Not much to do but get in trouble. *(pause)* You know what we did for fun on a Friday night when I was a kid? We used to go over to the junk yard... You know, Luciano's... and we used to smash old cars. Drink beer and smash cars.

MRS. WRIGHT: Sounds riveting.

MICK: I know right. Sometimes we would find a wrecked fancy car, like a Mercedes or something. That was a big deal, like a prize you know. Getting to destroy something nice like that.

MRS. WRIGHT: A Mercedes you say?

MICK: Yeah. Cool right?

MRS. WRIGHT: Was it dark blue?

MICK: Might have been.

MRS. WRIGHT: Well my husband drove the only Mercedes in Oakbranch. A dark blue one. He said the mayor of a town had to drive something nice or else people wouldn't look up to him. I told him, if he needed a car for that he wasn't a very good mayor. He didn't talk to me for two weeks after that. He still drove that damn Mercedes though. I hated that car. It was embarrassing. You smashed it you say?

MICK: Yeah. A couple guys would climb in first... sit in the back seat and pretend like they were being chauffeured around, all *(in a snooty voice)* "Shall we dine at the country club this evening?" and stuff. Then a couple of us would suddenly jump on the top of the car with big ol' steel pipes and start smashing it while they were still sitting in it. And they'd be all, "Oh Dear, Oh Dear. Hooligan's are smashing the Mercedes!" That was so fun.

MRS. WRIGHT: You smashed up the windows?

MICK: Oh yeah.

MRS. WRIGHT: And the head lights?

MICK: Of course. Anything that would break.

MRS. WRIGHT: How about where the driver sat?

MICK: Um. Probably.

MRS. WRIGHT: I can see the appeal.

MICK: It would always end with us getting chased off the property though. Old Mr. Luciano would come after us with his dog. Stupid fat little mutt. *(pause)* One time he almost got us too. We ran over by the glass, where the old bottles and stuff were, and we run right into a bunch of black kids who live over on the other side. They were throwing bottles at the building or something. We must have scared the... you know what out of them, coming around the corner like that carrying pipes. We were scared too, I ain't gonna lie. But they must have thought we were about to beat down on 'em. So one of 'em chucks a bottle right at me, and without even thinking, I keep my eye on the ball and... *(swings) Ka-chhhhhhhh!* Glass goes everywhere. And we just freeze. *(pause)* But then that stupid little mutt comes barking at us. So we ran one way and they ran the other. We saw 'em the next Monday in school. But it was like it never happened. We just acted like we were different people on Friday than we were on Monday, you know? *(pause)* Yep... that's what we did on a Friday night.

MRS. WRIGHT: Could have been worse I suppose.

MICK: Sometimes it was. So you ever wonder? You know… if you did good?

MRS. WRIGHT: I did my job well while the children were here. Then they were out of my hands. My influence ended when they left this school.

MICK: Well that ain't true Mrs. Wright. One time you said to me, "Mr. McCaffrey, you *probably* aren't stupid. You *definitely* aren't a genius, but you *probably* aren't stupid. And if you aren't stupid, then you can do things that aren't stupid." And you handed me my report card. Five B's and two C's. And you said, "A's are better, but B's will get you through college." *(pause)* I figured I'd farm oysters all my life like everybody else in my family. *(pause)* But last semester I got two A's and two B's in my college classes. I just thought you might want to know.

(MRS. WRIGHT stares at MICK. Long pause.)

MICK: *(looks at a photo)* Here's one from the olden days.

MRS. WRIGHT: The olden days huh?

MICK: Yeah. 1952. You know when I was a kid I used to think in the olden days, that everyone only wore black and white clothes. And I used to think they painted everything grey and that's why old pictures always looked like this.

MRS. WRIGHT: You thought that?

MICK: Yup.

MRS. WRIGHT: Well It's true.

MICK: What is?

MRS. WRIGHT: We painted everything gray.

MICK: Yeah right.

MRS. WRIGHT: Really we did. We just used black white and gray. We'd collect various dirts and what-not and mix them up to make paint. That's how it was in the "olden days". We used dirt for everything. And we couldn't afford new clothes so we just wore black and white so that the few clothes we had always matched.

MICK: You're a stinkin' Liar... ma'am.

MRS. WRIGHT: It's true. In the "olden days" it was very important that our clothes matched or else we'd be chased from the village with pitchforks and torches. *(pause)* Would I lie?

MICK: Aw Mrs. Wright I know you're lying! See? In the picture from the seventies your hair's brown. And to-day your hair is... *(pause, referring to her white hair)* a different shade of brown. But in the picture from 1952 your hair's grey just like everything else. That's proof that you are lying to me. I'm not stupid. You said so yourself.

MRS. WRIGHT: I said *probably* not stupid. *(smiles)*

MICK: Ha! Hey, you said something funny! I didn't know you could do that!

MRS. WRIGHT: Of course I can. I'm actually quite hysterical.

MICK: No way.

MRS. WRIGHT: Yes.

MICK: No way.

MRS. WRIGHT: Yes.

MICK: Show me. Tell me a joke.

MRS. WRIGHT: I don't know if I can think of any. My memory isn't as sharp as it used to be.

MICK: See.

MRS. WRIGHT: Oh and another thing, my memory isn't as sharp as it used to be.

MICK: *(pause)* Haaaa! I get it. That's not funny.

MRS. WRIGHT: Yes it is and you know it.

MICK: Not that funny.

MRS. WRIGHT: Yeah it was. Which class did you say that was?

MICK: "Mrs. Wright's fifth Grade Class"

MRS. WRIGHT: I mean what year?

MICK: Fifth! *(pause, realizing)* 1952

MRS. WRIGHT: Let me see it.

MICK: Say please.

MRS. WRIGHT: Excuse me?

MICK: You always use to say manners are a-

MRS. WRIGHT: Give it to me! *(takes photo)*

MICK: Look at you. You were pretty back then. *(catching himself)* Almost as pretty as you are now. *(pause)* Who's that in the back?

MRS. WRIGHT: That's Bo's wife. Her name was Marian.

MICK: Everybody knows Bo's wife's name was Marian. He talks about her all the time. He tell you about fixing the light bulb?

(The lights flicker on and the sounds of electricity as ARTHUR has repaired the generator. The record player accelerates to full speed children's music.)

MICK: Heeeeeyyyy!

MRS. WRIGHT: Bravo!

ARTHUR: *(from offstage)* THAT'S RIGHT! THIS HERE IS BO WELLS' HOUSE! *(enters, then in the style of a preacher)* And Bo Wells said, "LET THERE BE LIGHT!" and there was light! And Bo saw the light! And Delores saw the light! And Mick saw the light! And the light was goooooooooood! The light was what?! *(no response)* The light was what?! *(points to MICK)*

MICK: Good?

ARTHUR: The light was what?! *(points to MICK)*

MICK: *(joining the celebration)* The light was gooooood!

(ARTHUR crosses to the radiator and feels it.)

ARTHUR: Ahhhhh… And Bo Wells said, "LET THERE BE HEAT!" and there was Heat! And Bo felt the heat. And Delores felt the heat. And Mick felt the heat! And the heat was what?!

MICK: The heat was goooooooood!

ARTHUR: The heat was what?! *(points to MRS. WRIGHT, no response.)* The heat was what?! *(points to MRS. WRIGHT)*

MRS. WRIGHT: *(dryly)* Good.

MICK: Say it sister!

ARTHUR: That's right! The heat was goooooooooood! And Bo said *(points to the record player)* "Let there be music!" And there was music! And the music was… *(pause, dances, stops)* That music's no good. Ain't nothing but kid's stuff. *(shuts off record player)* Now that generator, that weren't no kid's stuff! That was some serious fixin' that had to happen down there. Froze solid that thing was. All rusted-up. I got it though. Lubed it, banged it with a hammer, and then I got the *big* hammer! I got it goin'. Bring on the love people. Bring on the love!

MRS. WRIGHT: All you did was bang it with a hammer?

ARTHUR: Yeah so what?

MRS. WRIGHT: What's so impressive about that?

ARTHUR: We got heat didn't we?

MRS. WRIGHT: Yes but you are acting like you discovered fire or something.

ARTHUR: You have heat five minutes ago?

MRS. WRIGHT: Obviously not.

ARTHUR: You got heat now?

MRS. WRIGHT: Yes.

ARTHUR: Then I *did* discover fire! *(laughs)*

MRS. WRIGHT: I'm just saying it wasn't such a big deal. Any one of us could have banged on that old generator.

ARTHUR: *(serious)* You think so? Where?

MRS. WRIGHT: What do you mean where?

ARTHUR: Where would you have banged it?

MICK: Bo, she would have banged it in the basement. That's where the generator is.

ARTHUR: Shut up Mick! I mean which part of the generator would you hit? You hit the wrong part, and you break the whole thing. Where'd you hit it?

MRS. WRIGHT: I'm sure I'd figure it out. Couldn't be too hard.

ARTHUR: What you mean it couldn't be too hard? What you mean by that?

MICK: She means maybe it's not that hard. I mean, if it was hard you could still fix it but maybe this time it really wasn't so hard-

ARTHUR: Shut up Mick! What you mean Delores? Couldn't be too hard?

MRS. WRIGHT: Nothing.

ARTHUR: You mean if I could do it? You mean, it couldn't be too hard if I could do it? *(abruptly exits towards basement)*

MRS. WRIGHT: Of course not.

ARTHUR: *(yelling from offstage)* Alright then! Let's see!

MRS. WRIGHT: You are being ridiculous Bo! No need to make a scene over it! I was just... I didn't mean anything by it. I was just-

(The sounds of banging. The lights flicker off.)

MRS. WRIGHT: Bo?!

MICK: Awe man what you have to go and do that for? Come on man. It's freezing. Turn it back on.

MRS. WRIGHT: *(overlapping)* That is childish. I swear you are worse than those children. A grown man, acting like a child like this.

ARTHUR: *(offstage)* ALRIGHT... NOW DELORES... YOU GO DISCOVER FIRE!

MRS. WRIGHT: Don't be silly Bo. Can you please-

MICK: Really Bo, I think she got the point-

ARTHUR: *(enters)* No no Delores, grab a couple of
sticks or something and rub them together real hard
and build us a big ol' fire.

MRS. WRIGHT: Will you please just turn the gen-

ARTHUR: Yeah, we can make a big ol' bonfire and
dance around it and celebrate when Delores discovered fire for the world!

MRS. WRIGHT: Fine. I used the wrong words. I should
have kept my mouth shut. Now can you please turn the
heat back on?

ARTHUR: But Delores, the heat *is* on. Problem is, the
generator done went and broke! Imagine that!

MRS. WRIGHT: It did not. You simply shut it off.

ARTHUR: Nah, it's broke now. I used that same hammer
and I hit it in the wrong place. And now I went and
broke it! And I just can't figure out how to fix it. It's
just way too complicated for my little brain. We need
you to go down and figure it out for us.

MICK: I'll go fix it-

ARTHUR: Like hell you will! Sit down Mick! *(to MRS.
WRIGHT)* Will you please go make fire for us? The
hammer's down there waitin' for you. We're likely to
freeze to death if you don't save us. *Help* us Delores.
Help us.

MRS. WRIGHT: Fine I will. *(exits)*

72

ARTHUR: Yeah... Good luck lady! Don't hurt yourself!

MICK: Come on Bo. She didn't mean anything by it.

ARTHUR: I don't need some old lady who think she the queen of Oakbranch trying to knock me down.

MICK: She wasn't knocking-

ARTHUR: Hell yes she was! She been treating me like her "boy" since 1952 and I done run out of "Yes Ma'am's".

MICK: You think she can even swing that hammer?

ARTHUR: Of course she can't swing it! It's a 10 pound sledge hammer. She can't even pick it up! If I thought she could swing it, I wouldn't let her anywhere near that generator.

(MRS. WRIGHT re-enters.)

ARTHUR: Speak of the devil! What's the matter devil? Couldn't rub those sticks together fast enough to make fire? You gotta really put your back into it! *(laughs)*

MRS. WRIGHT: I just-

ARTHUR: Or maybe you just need a bigger hammer to beat on that generator with. Or how about that paddle? I hear you can swing that real hard.

MRS. WRIGHT: It's not that. I just-

ARTHUR: What is it then? Can't figure out the generator? Can't figure out what's what? Don't know where to hit it?

MRS. WRIGHT: I can't go down the stairs! OK? *(pause)* I am happy to go down there to start the generator again, but I just... can't make it down the stairs. They are too steep and I don't think I can.

ARTHUR: *(long pause)* Mick. Go turn it on. The switch is on the side.

MICK: OK.

ARTHUR: And when you're done, go outside and shovel out Delores's car. The driveway too. All the way to the road. As soon as that plow truck come by, we are getting out of here.

MICK: By myself? That'll take half the night. *(pause)* Fine. *(exits)*

MRS. WRIGHT: I just couldn't make it down the stairs. I just can't do that anymore. It happens to everybody at some point. Soon you'll be looking at a set of stairs and you too will start wondering if you will be dead before you get to the other end. *(beat)* Well that's where I am. It's like my whole life has been a giant set of stairs that I have been climbing. But, suddenly, I start to wobble and I realize that if I take one more step, I'm likely to stumble and crash all the way down to where I started. Helpless. I am not interested in being an infant... one of those sorry old ladies who sit around the nursing home waiting for somebody to change their undergarments. You understand me?

ARTHUR: *(pause)* Sit down then. You ain't never gonna be in a nursing home. Besides, what nurse would ever survive comin' to work with you every day? Huh?

MRS. WRIGHT: You did.

ARTHUR: I know, but it almost killed me. Now... no point in tiring out those legs. They got you this far, they earned a rest. Have a seat now and don't be stubborn.

(The lights come on. MRS. WRIGHT continues to stand.)

MICK: *(from offstage)* GOT IT!

ARTHUR: I said sit down.

MRS. WRIGHT: I'm fine standing.

ARTHUR: Well I ain't. I'm tired. I need to sit. *(pause)* I'd appreciate it if you'd keep me company.

(ARTHUR sits.)

MRS. WRIGHT: *(pause)* Fine. *(She sits.)*

(Blackout)

ACT 2, SCENE 2

(ARTHUR and MRS. WRIGHT are playing dominos. AR-THUR skillfully holds his tiles. MRS. WRIGHT has her tiles arranged neatly on the table.)

ARTHUR: You gonna play or what?

MRS. WRIGHT: I'm strategizing.

ARTHUR: Strategizing? I just taught you to play. What kinds a strategy you think you got?

MRS. WRIGHT: You beat me four games already. I have to do something. No point in playing if there's no competition. *(plays a tile gently)*

ARTHUR: What was that?

MRS. WRIGHT: I played my tile.

ARTHUR: How many times I gotta tell you?

MRS. WRIGHT: You play your way and I'll play my way.

ARTHUR: Your way's no good. This ain't no old lady game. If you're gonna play dominos then you gotta play it right.

MRS. WRIGHT: I don't like your way. It's too aggressive.

ARTHUR: Oh please. Just watch how I do it. Gotta put your heart into it.

(ARTHUR slams a Domino with great gusto and flair.)

ARTHUR: There it is! What do you think of that?
(laughs)

MRS. WRIGHT: I think it's silly. Why do you have to slam it down like that?

ARTHUR: You just do. It's part of the game.

(MRS. WRIGHT plays a tile with exaggerated daintiness)

MRS. WRIGHT: A two... and a six.

ARTHUR: I ain't gonna play any more dominos with you if you gonna turn it into an old lady game.

MRS. WRIGHT: Fine. Then after this we are going to play cribbage.

ARTHUR: Cribbage? What the hell is cribbage?

MRS. WRIGHT: It's just a card game.

ARTHUR: I don't play card games. Card games are for housewives and fat men who never leave their lazy-boy.

MRS. WRIGHT: Excuse me?

ARTHUR: I just don't play cards. Cards are no good. When we play dominos, everybody's part of it, see. We play outside. People stand around and watch. Over in front of the Stop'n'Stop.

MRS. WRIGHT: In front of the what?

ARTHUR: Stop'n'Stop.

MRS. WRIGHT: What's a "stop and stop"?

ARTHUR: It's a store. "Louisa's Stop'n'Stop."

MRS. WRIGHT: That's the name?

ARTHUR: Yeah.

MRS. WRIGHT: Well that doesn't make any sense. Maybe "Stop and *Shop*" or "Stop and *Go*". But "Stop and *Stop*"? It doesn't make any sense at all.

ARTHUR: You never been to the Stop'n'Stop?

MRS. WRIGHT: I don't get to that part of town very often.

ARTHUR: It's like a 7-11 only better. It's all we got in my part of town. Ain't no real grocery store anywhere around. But I ain't complaining. Miss Louisa makes some good bar-be-cue. *(slams a tile)* Can't win on that, suckah! Can't win on that!

MRS. WRIGHT: What did you call me?

ARTHUR: Suckah. Just part of the game. See, you ain't getting' it. In our neighborhood it's where we see each other... tell jokes. It's where I win at dominos. See? "Stop" what you're doin'... then "stop" in to Miss Louisa's for a while and see a few friends. Stop... and Stop. And nobody's playin' cards there either. Can't lay cards out in front of the store. The wind'll blow 'em away. That's why we play dominos. Cards are no fun anyhow.

MRS. WRIGHT: Well cards are no different than dominos. It's just numbers on little rectangles. It's not difficult. You can do it.

ARTHUR: I know I can do it! I just don't play cards! I play the bones… throw the stones. I'm the best player in my whole neighborhood. I win seven outa ten every time. That's no lie neither.

MRS. WRIGHT: You're just afraid I'd beat you.

ARTHUR: Afraid? Afraid YOU'D beat ME? Shoot. I ain't afraid you'd beat me. I KNOW you'd beat me. I just said I don't… play… cards. I always get the black cards mixed up. What the hell are they anyway? A club? A spade? What the hell are they? At least the red ones look like what they are. A heart look like a heart. A diamond look like a diamond. What the hell's a spade anyway?

MRS. WRIGHT: *(focused on her dominoes)* It's a shovel.

ARTHUR: A shovel? It don't look anything like a shovel.

MRS. WRIGHT: Sure it does. It looks like a little garden spade. The kind with the little handle and a pointed end.

ARTHUR: You sure that's what it is?

MRS. WRIGHT: No. I made that up. I have no Idea what it is. It's just a suit.

ARTHUR: Are you gonna play a bone or are you just gonna sit there?

MRS. WRIGHT: I'm still strategizing.

ARTHUR: What you strategizing about? You only got two left. Pick one.

MRS. WRIGHT: Can I add three dots and three dots together so I can play it on that six?

ARTHUR: No.

MRS. WRIGHT: Oh. OK then.

(MRS. WRIGHT plays a tile.)

ARTHUR: You are the worst dominos player I know.

MRS. WRIGHT: Why? What was wrong with that?

ARTHUR: You just told me what you had in your hand. You asked if you could add a three and a three.

MRS. WRIGHT: So?

ARTHUR: That means you got double threes.

MRS. WRIGHT: How do you know? Maybe I was just strategizing.

ARTHUR: Maybe you just told me what you have in your hand. Now I know you got nothing but threes. So now I'ma play over here and block that one right there. Now you can't play it anywhere. HA!

(ARTHUR plays a tile. MRS. WRIGHT immediately slams a tile down on the six with great flair.)

MRS. WRIGHT: DOMINO, SUCKAH!

ARTHUR: What you just do?! What do you mean Domino? How'd you-

MRS. WRIGHT: I was strategizing!

ARTHUR: Aw lady, you a cheater!

MRS. WRIGHT: Just part of the game!

ARTHUR: You a sneak! Just like Marian. You a sneak! *(scowls)* I still won you four outa five. Don't you forget that.

MRS. WRIGHT: I'm sure you won't let me forget it.

ARTHUR: But I ain't lying. You are just like Marian. Stubborn and sneaky. Never could figure you out. You two are like those cards. You the club and she the spade. Don't make no sense.

MRS. WRIGHT: That's probably why we didn't like each other.

ARTHUR: *(mixing the tiles)* Prob'ly. And just like you, she always in charge. If I raised my voice... she'd drown me out with hers and I'd quiet down quick. And God forbid I raised my hand... One time, just one time, I raised up my hand to her. Didn't get it past my shoulder before the next thing I know, I got a cantaloupe across my head. From then on, she always kept one fresh melon in the ice box. And every time I get brave, out come the melon. She put it gently on the table and say in the sweetest voice, "I'm sorry Baby, what were you sayin'? I was busy thinkin' about what I could do with this delicious cantaloupe." Yeah, I got the point.

81

MRS. WRIGHT: Maybe I should have tried that. The cantaloupe. I used a mixing spoon. A slotted one. And it wasn't just once. Right across the face. A regular spoon was too smooth. But the slotted one had nice little ridges on it. For a week after, my husband would hear, "Mayor Wright, what happened to you?" And he'd always say, "My damn neighbor's dog again... clawed me right across the face. But that's alright. It's just one of God's creatures." He always could make his screw-ups sound good. Always came out on top.

ARTHUR: Not this time though.

MRS. WRIGHT: What do you mean by that?

ARTHUR: You're on top now and he's down there in the dirt somewhere. Sometimes it just comes down to not dyin'. *(pause)* I always thought you two were peas in a pod. The mayor and first lady.

MRS. WRIGHT: Not everyone finds their Marian, Bo. Some people get stuck with an Edward.

ARTHUR: Yeah... or an Arthur. Too bad for them, huh?

MRS. WRIGHT: Yes, too bad. *(long pause)* How about Wells Elementary?

ARTHUR: Excuse me?

MRS. WRIGHT: The new school. I want to name it Wells Elementary School.

ARTHUR: That's crazy.

MRS. WRIGHT: It was always my choice, from the start. That's why I asked you to do this with me.

ARTHUR: Well, I never considered for a second that the school might be named Wells Elementary. The thought never even crossed my mind.

MRS. WRIGHT: I think it is a fitting name.

ARTHUR: Are you lying to me? You tryin' to get back at me for the generator thing? Because that ain't funny if you are.

MRS. WRIGHT: I'm not lying.

ARTHUR: Well... if that's what you want... I'm not gonna get in the way... But I'm not sure the city would agree to naming it that.

MRS. WRIGHT: Oh who cares about the city. I'm paying for the school. I name it whatever I want to name it and they'll shut up about it.

ARTHUR: Arthur Wells Elementary? That's crazy. I'm just a-

MRS. WRIGHT: Arthur Wells? That *is* crazy. I don't want to name it after you. I want to name it after your wife. Marian Wells Elementary.

ARTHUR: *(pause)* You want to name it after Marian?

MRS. WRIGHT: I do.

ARTHUR: Yes! I mean... Yes! Please do! Name it after Marian, Delores. You *gotta* name it after her! *(beat)* But you better make it a beautiful school if you gonna put her name on it!

MRS. WRIGHT: Oh we will. You should see it. It's a spectacular design.

ARTHUR: But, why Marian? You didn't even like her.

MRS. WRIGHT: Can we just leave it? Can we just name the school and be happy with that?

ARTHUR: *(pause)* Just leave it?

MRS. WRIGHT: Yes.

ARTHUR: *(long pause)* No, I don't think we can.

MRS. WRIGHT: You don't?

ARTHUR: No. *(pause)* You're strategizing aren't you?

MRS. WRIGHT: Bo, I'm offering something very special for you... and for Marian.

ARTHUR: Marian ain't here. *(pause)* And I worked for you for most of my life and you never gave me nothin'. Why you doin' this?

MRS. WRIGHT: I just thought Marian was a good choice.

ARTHUR: Why?

MRS. WRIGHT: She was a teacher.

ARTHUR: So?

MRS. WRIGHT: And she was a good teacher.

ARTHUR: So?

MRS. WRIGHT: And she was the first... African American teacher at this-

ARTHUR: I told you, they wouldn't let her be a teacher!

MRS. WRIGHT: Fine. She was the first employee at this school.

ARTHUR: It don't make no sense. You up to something. You are strategizing. Why'd you pick her?

MRS. WRIGHT: I just told you-

ARTHUR: I'm tired of you yankin' my chain.

MRS. WRIGHT: Why are being like this?

ARTHUR: Why'd you pick her?

MRS. WRIGHT: Bo, I just-

ARTHUR: And don't you lie to me. You think I'm too stupid to know what's goin' on? I seen this from the minute you walked in here.

MRS. WRIGHT: What is it that you think is going on?

ARTHUR: Don't make me say it Delores. You know why you are here. Why does a rich, old, tired lady drive herself all the way to this here school? A lady who can barely walk, and even more dangerous in her car. Just to talk about what to name a school? I don't think so.

MRS. WRIGHT: Then what is it Bo? What is this rich tired old lady standing here for? Offering a gift for you and for your wife. What is so horrible about that?

ARTHUR: You're sick aren't you? And you're prob'ly gonna die.

MRS. WRIGHT: We are all going to die.

ARTHUR: I mean soon.

MRS. WRIGHT: Like you said, I'm an old lady, right?

ARTHUR: And you wanna go to your grave in peace. *(pause)* What happened Delores? What did you do?

MRS. WRIGHT: I didn't do anything.

ARTHUR: You did. You did something. What did you do?

MRS. WRIGHT: I didn't do anything!

ARTHUR: WHAT DID YOU DO?!

MRS. WRIGHT: *(pause, softly)* Nothing.

ARTHUR: You still doin' nothin' then. Whatever you did, or whatever you didn't... you still doin' it. Go to the grave with that. *(pause)* And keep your damn school. Name it after yourself. You can put a statue out front. You just sittin' there... doin' *nothin'*. *(pause)* I'm leavin'. I wanna go home. *(He begins to leave.)*

MRS. WRIGHT: *(pause, as ARTHUR reaches the door)* I wanted to stop them!

(ARTHUR stops. Long pause)

MRS. WRIGHT: They called us here to the school. Edward said we had to come. He said a couple of the parents, fathers, needed to speak with the Mayor, and with me. They were angry. One of the girls from the class said something to her mother and the word spread like a fire. Word was... Marian had beaten a white child.

ARTHUR: It was because that child needed to be hit!

MRS. WRIGHT: When we arrived, the school was empty, dark. The paddle was still on the floor in the middle of the room. Right there. They didn't like that one bit. It set them off when they saw that paddle. I tried to explain that I had her fired-

ARTHUR: *You* fired her?

MRS. WRIGHT: I told them she was gone and their children had nothing to worry about, and they should leave her alone. But that wasn't enough.

ARTHUR: You should have stopped them Delores.

MRS. WRIGHT: It was too fast. She showed up. She was angry. She had been drinking and she was screaming at the school. I don't think she even knew we were in here, but she was yelling like we were. That's when it happened.

ARTHUR: I don't want to hear it any more.

MRS. WRIGHT: They didn't mean for it to end like that.

ARTHUR: I said I don't want to hear it Delores!

MRS. WRIGHT: It just, it just got out of control.

ARTHUR: Delores, you keep it to yourself. You been keeping it to yourself for fifty years!

MRS. WRIGHT: They just wanted to warn her. They called her things and they threatened things but they never meant it. They just wanted her to know. It was not OK. Not from her. Not their children. But-

ARTHUR: But they didn't stop there, right?

MRS. WRIGHT: No. That's when everything went wrong. They dragged her down to the river, but like you said, she was afraid... afraid to go near the water. So she started to flail and scream. She wasn't afraid of the men, she just didn't want to go near that water. But that just encouraged them. "Take her to the river!" they yelled. "I think you need a bath. Time to wash that dirt off your face." They carried her past the oak tree, by the rope swing. The water was way down. It was low tide see. So they walked through the mud, towards the water. Their feet were sinking deep. But she kept kicking and she kept fighting them. Until one of the men grabbed the swing and wrapped it around her feet, to keep her in control. But she was a fighter. She pushed herself free and fell from their arms, but she was already tied. Her ankle was already tied up in the rope and she was just... hanging there. Her head just barely touched the water and she screamed. It was like that water was boiling and it hurt every time she touched it.

ARTHUR: She was afraid of the water.

MRS. WRIGHT: Then Edward said, "Come on Delores. This isn't our problem... This isn't our problem," he said... "The Mayor can't be here for this. She'll learn her lesson and she'll be alright." And he took me by the arm and we climbed into our car, and we drove home.

ARTHUR: And you left them there to kill her.

MRS. WRIGHT: No! Nobody wanted to do that. We just drove away. And...

ARTHUR: And what?

MRS. WRIGHT: And they... The fathers...

ARTHUR: What?

MRS. WRIGHT: They left her there.

ARTHUR: Hangin' by her ankle.

MRS. WRIGHT: Yes.

ARTHUR: Over the river.

MRS. WRIGHT: Yes.

ARTHUR: Her head touching the water.

MRS. WRIGHT: Yes.

ARTHUR: *(long pause)* The tide was coming in Delores.

MRS. WRIGHT: It was. They weren't thinking. *(beat)* They forgot about the tide. *(long pause)* I'm sorry.

(ARTHUR picks up the paddle.)

ARTHUR: YOU SORRY?! You sorry for what?! You did nothin', right? Said so yourself. You didn't put her in the water. You didn't tie her to that rope. You didn't even make her come to work at this here school. You would have sent her right back to the colored school if you had your way. You did nothin', right? Because you a good lady, right? You been takin' care of this here town for your whole life. You gotta be good, because they don't name a street after you unless you good. And they don't name a, a park after you unless you *real* good. And I'm pretty sure you gonna have a school named after you. When your time come, you can just sit up there at the right hand of God and shine your light down on Oakbranch and the whole wide world, because you did... nothin'.

MRS. WRIGHT: *(quietly)* I stopped her.

ARTHUR: You stopped who?

MRS. WRIGHT: Marian.

ARTHUR: But she-

MRS. WRIGHT: She never hit him.

ARTHUR: What do you mean-

MRS. WRIGHT: I did. I paddled that child instead. It wasn't Marian.

ARTHUR: You?

MRS. WRIGHT: Yes. He was bullying that boy. The little boy from the colored school.

ARTHUR: You did?

MRS. WRIGHT: That's right.

ARTHUR: Because he was picking on a black child?

MRS. WRIGHT: Because he was picking on a child! A small child. A frightened child. Nothing else mattered.

ARTHUR: And so you hit him.

MRS. WRIGHT: Yes. But she was going to! She might as well have! She had the paddle in one hand and his arm in the other. She was going to!

ARTHUR: Until you stopped her.

MRS. WRIGHT: Yes! I knew something would happen. Her hitting that boy. So I sent the children out of the room. I didn't want them to see. She was angry. But there is a line! There... *was* a line back then. A line that couldn't be crossed. I was protecting her.

ARTHUR: Well you did a fine job.

MRS. WRIGHT: I was *trying* to protect her.

ARTHUR: Were you?

MRS. WRIGHT: Yes.

ARTHUR: Or was it that other thing?

MRS. WRIGHT: What thing?

ARTHUR: The line. The line she was about to cross. "Not in my school" you thought. "Hell no, not in my school. Not her."

MRS. WRIGHT: She wasn't thinking.

ARTHUR: She got some nerve, right?

MRS. WRIGHT: She was being reckless! A danger to herself. Out of control.

ARTHUR: Ooh yeah... Like a wild animal.

MRS. WRIGHT: I didn't say that. She was just upset. So I stepped in-

ARTHUR: Tamed the beast!

MRS. WRIGHT: I was protecting her!

ARTHUR: The great hunter Delores!

MRS. WRIGHT: I closed the door. It was just me, Marian and the boy and I warned him that if he told his father, that he'd get an even bigger beating from him. I thought that would quiet things down. Then I took that paddle from Marian... and I struck the child.

ARTHUR: So they fired you right?

MRS. WRIGHT: No.

ARTHUR: Then that night you got dragged down to the river right?

MRS. WRIGHT: What? No.

ARTHUR: And they hung you up like an animal after the kill. Ready to carve you up. How'd that feel? Getting' strung up like that?

MRS. WRIGHT: Bo.

ARTHUR: How'd that rope feel around your leg?! And how'd it feel when they swung you out on that rope swing, and your head splash through the river?! Then the tide start to rise... inch... by inch. Your face under the water. The water that makes you so scared you can't breathe just thinking about it! Then how long were you able to... How long could hold your head up... hold it up... out of the water so you could... *(pause, broken)* so she could breathe before she got so tired she couldn't do it no more?! Huh?! Tell me! *(quietly)* Tell me how that felt Delores.

MRS. WRIGHT: I don't know.

(MRS. WRIGHT moves to hug ARTHUR. ARTHUR stops her. The paddle remains tightly in his hand.)

MRS. WRIGHT: I'm not that person Bo. Not anymore. I'm not that person who let that happen.

(ARTHUR steps back and looks her close in the face.)

ARTHUR: Part of you is.

MRS. WRIGHT: *(nods, pause)* OK. Part of me is. But most of me is not that person. *(pause)* Do you see that?

ARTHUR: No I don't. *(pause)* But Marian would. *(He hands the paddle to MRS. WRIGHT and steps away. Long pause. He is numb, distant.)* What happened to that little boy? The one who was being bullied? You know what come of him?

MRS. WRIGHT: Yes.

ARTHUR: So what happened to him?

MRS. WRIGHT: He passed away a few years ago.

ARTHUR: He's dead? That little boy?

MRS. WRIGHT: He was over fifty. He had a bad heart. He always was frail.

ARTHUR: He was?

MRS. WRIGHT: But he did OK. He went to college. He had a family.

ARTHUR: Well that's good. Family's good.

MRS. WRIGHT: Bo... I just wanted to tell you... I just wanted to say-

ARTHUR: Aw Delores, I don't need any of that. It don't matter now.

MRS. WRIGHT: But-

ARTHUR: Maybe one of these days you can show me how to make that omelet. Show me how to do it the way Marian used to, like you said you could. It makes me hungry just thinking about it. You think there's any more of them cookies in the kitchen?

MRS. WRIGHT: Cookies?

ARTHUR: Yeah. I'm starvin'. I could use somethin' right now. Would you mind lookin'?

MRS. WRIGHT: But-

ARTHUR: Please Delores.

MRS. WRIGHT: *(pause)* OK Bo.

(MRS. WRIGHT exits to the kitchen. ARTHUR picks up Marian's class photo. He examines it. A rush of emotion. Blackout)

ACT 2, SCENE 3

(One week later. The classroom is entirely empty except for one chair. MICK enters. He wears a brown suit and a crooked clip-on bowtie. He straightens up his suit. He calls offstage.)

MICK: I'm back! Are you ready to go?! *(pause)* You gotta take a look at me. I shine up real good! *(pause)* Thanks for letting me borrow this suit. *(pause)* It starts in half an hour! You ready? *(pause)* I did everything you told me to do! *(pause)* If you... need more time... alone... I can wait in the car.

(MRS. WRIGHT enters. Her walking is labored. She carries but does not use her cane. She is dressed formally.)

MRS. WRIGHT: I was just checking the locks. Making sure all was secure.

MICK: What are you doing that for? They are knocking this building down tomorrow. Nothing left to steal. And how many times do I gotta tell you, use your cane Mrs. Wright.

MRS. WRIGHT: I told you, you can call me Delores.

MICK: Use your cane Delores! Just be careful, OK?

MRS. WRIGHT: *(seeing MICK)* That suit, it... suits you.

MICK: Ha! That's not funny... And thanks. You sure it's OK?... I mean, that I'm wearing it?

MRS. WRIGHT: Of course. It has just been collecting dust in my husband's closet. You can keep it. It looks better on you anyway.

MICK: Thanks... Thank you. *(pause)* I have your car outside, shined up real nice, like you asked. Sorry it took me so long. There was a line over at the car wash. Everybody was cleaning up for the funeral, and I mean everybody. Miss Louisa wanted me to tell you that she was having a bar-be-que thing over at the Stop'n'Stop after. She wanted me to invite you to come. She said it would be an honor. I guess the whole neighborhood's gonna be there.

MRS. WRIGHT: I don't know where it is.

MICK: It's OK. I can get us there.

MRS. WRIGHT: Alright then.

MICK: The sun's out. Warm too. Probably won't need that coat.

MRS. WRIGHT: I'll keep it on. It will serve as extra padding in case I fall.

MICK: Yeah OK. But don't worry, I won't let you fall. *(beat)* I never thought I'd see the sun after all that snow... or the roads for that matter. It's almost all melted now. Only took a week. *(pause)* Hey did you see this? Look. *(shows his bowtie)* They were passing them out over at the car wash. You know, like Bo wore. Everybody decided we'd all wear bowties. That was a good idea. Wish I thought of it. But I didn't have one. So they gave me this one over at the car wash. Looks like Bo's, right? Except he probably tied his. This is just a clip-on. Which is good, because I have no idea how to do up one of these.

MRS. WRIGHT: Come here. You look a mess. Don't you know how to dress yourself?

MICK: Is it crooked?

(MRS. WRIGHT removes MICK's bowtie.)

MRS. WRIGHT: Check your inside pocket.

(He does and pulls out a real bow tie. MRS. WRIGHT takes it and begins to tie it on MICK.)

MICK: How'd you know about it? I mean how'd you know everybody was wearing bowties today?

(MRS. WRIGHT continues to tie and smiles.)

MICK: It was your idea wasn't it? You are sneaky. That was a good idea.

MRS. WRIGHT: Did you deliver that letter like I asked?

MICK: Yes I did.

MRS. WRIGHT: You put it right in his hand? You put it right in the Mayor's hand and you said, "This is a-"

MICK: "This is a letter from Delores Wright instructing you to preserve the old oak tree over by the river when the new school is built."

MRS. WRIGHT: And the other part?

MICK: Yes, and I told him if he didn't that you would take all your money out of the new school and give it to whoever was gonna run against him in the next election.

MRS. WRIGHT: Good. *(pause)* Well, no sense hanging around here any longer. It's nothing but bricks and wood now. The heart of this place has stopped beating. *(long pause)* It was a lot of work wasn't it? Clearing it out? Generations of children, and teachers. It must have been hard getting rid of all that history.

MICK: Yeah it was. Especially without Bo. They gave me some young guy to help out. But you know how kids are. All he ever did was ask questions. Slow as molasses too, I'll tell you what.

MRS. WRIGHT: *(chuckles)* I heard Bo say that once.

MICK: Really? About who?

MRS. WRIGHT: I don't remember.

MICK: Oh.

MRS. WRIGHT: Mick?

MICK: Yeah?

MRS. WRIGHT: Thanks for driving me today.

MICK: It's OK.

MRS. WRIGHT: I just needed somebody… to drive me… that's all. I don't think I can do it anymore. I'm too… old. I don't get out very often, so it doesn't really matter.

MICK: Well I can drive you anytime you want. Take you out to lunch.

MRS. WRIGHT: Thank you Mick.

MICK: You know you got that ground breaking ceremony in the spring. The one for the new school. I
could drive you to that.

MRS. WRIGHT: The spring? I don't think I'll... Fine.
You can even use the shovel for me. I don't think I
could handle it.

MICK: They gonna have a gold shovel, right?

MRS. WRIGHT: I imagine. Yes, I'll make sure of it.

MICK: Well then it's a good thing I have this suit. I gotta
look good next to that shovel. What are you gonna say
in your speech?

MRS. WRIGHT: I'm not making a speech.

MICK: You gotta make a speech. You're the guest of
honor.

MRS. WRIGHT: You think so?

MICK: Yup. You gotta look good and you gotta make a
speech.

MRS. WRIGHT: Well then, I don't know. You can help
me write something.

MICK: OK. We got plenty of time. Spring is a long time
from now.

MRS. WRIGHT: Yes it is. *(pause)* But if for some reason
I can't make it to the ceremony, I'll tell them you can
make that speech for me.

MICK: Yeah right. I said I'd drive you. It's no problem at
all.

MRS. WRIGHT: *(pause)* So... what did he look like Mick? When you found him. What... How was he?

MICK: He actually looked pretty good. I was putting the shovel away and I saw him sitting over by the tree. He was just leaning there, in the middle of all that snow, like it was a summer day. Like he was just waiting there. And he was smiling like he always did. So I said, "Hey Bo. What are you doing out here?" And that's when I realized. I guess the cold got 'em. Five minutes later, that old plow truck came by. If Bo had just waited a little while longer.

MRS. WRIGHT: I don't think he wanted to wait. He waited long enough. *(pause)* You know I had a dream about him last night. He and I were sitting under that oak tree, next to that old black scar. It was a beautiful summer day and we were just sitting there playing dominos. He was winning, but I didn't care. I was enjoying the company. And I look up at the tree and I see that old rope swing. And Marian is sitting there, watching us play dominoes from that old rope swing. She is giving me a dirty look, but I am still glad to see her. Birds are singing, children are laughing and I can hear the sounds of the river going by as the tide goes out to sea. But then the skies go dark and the wind begins to blow. And suddenly Marian is being blown around by the storm so hard, but she holds on tight. She is a fighter. So I turn to Bo and say, "Bo, do something! She is going to fall into the river! Catch her!" But he isn't there. And next thing I know, he is sitting up on that branch, and he has the rope from her rope swing in his hand and he says to Marian, "Don't worry kiddo, Bo got you. Bo Wells knows how to make a rope swing." And he did.

(Blackout. END OF PLAY.)

101

ADDENDUM

Dominoes set-up for top of Act 2 Scene 2:

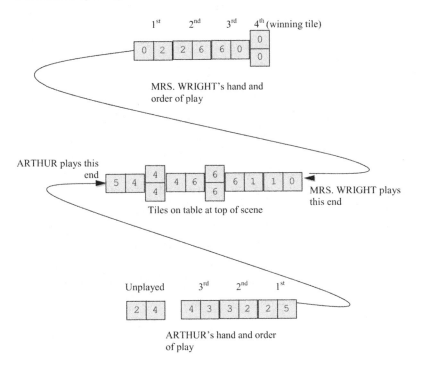

1st   2nd   3rd   4th (winning tile)

MRS. WRIGHT's hand and
order of play

ARTHUR plays this
end

MRS. WRIGHT plays
this end

Tiles on table at top of scene

Unplayed   3rd   2nd   1st

ARTHUR's hand and order
of play

Extra dominoes should lie face-down making up the "boneyard".

Made in the USA
Coppell, TX
16 December 2022